Bible Study for Kids

A Fun, Easy-to-Read Guide with Simple Explanations and Big Lessons to Help Kids Grow in Faith

© Copyright 2025 - All rights reserved.

The content contained within this book may not be reproduced, duplicated, or transmitted without direct written permission from the author or the publisher.

Under no circumstances will any blame or legal responsibility be held against the publisher, or author, for any damages, reparation, or monetary loss due to the information contained within this book, either directly or indirectly.

Legal Notice:

This book is copyright protected. It is only for personal use. You cannot amend, distribute, sell, use, quote, or paraphrase any part, or the content within this book, without the consent of the author or publisher.

Disclaimer Notice:

Please note the information contained within this document is for educational and entertainment purposes only. All effort has been executed to present accurate, up-to-date, reliable, and complete information. No warranties of any kind are declared or implied. Readers acknowledge that the author is not engaging in the rendering of legal, financial, medical, or professional advice. The content within this book has been derived from various sources. Please consult a licensed professional before attempting any techniques outlined in this book.

By reading this document, the reader agrees that under no circumstances is the author responsible for any losses, direct or indirect, that are incurred as a result of the use of the information contained within this document, including, but not limited to, errors, omissions, or inaccuracies.

Welcome Aboard, Check Out This Limited-Time Free Bonus!

Ahoy, reader! Welcome to the Ahoy Publications family, and thanks for snagging a copy of this book! Since you've chosen to join us on this journey, we'd like to offer you something special.

Check out the link below for a FREE e-book filled with delightful facts about American History.

But that's not all - you'll also have access to our exclusive email list with even more free e-books and insider knowledge. Well, what are ye waiting for? Click the link below to join and set sail toward exciting adventures in American History.

Access your bonus here
https://ahoypublications.com/
Or, Scan the QR code!

Table of Contents

- PART 1: DISCOVERING GOD'S TRUTH IN HIS WORD 1
  - CHAPTER 1: WELCOME TO YOUR BIBLE ADVENTURE!........................3
  - CHAPTER 2: THE BIBLE: GOD'S OWN WORD 6
  - CHAPTER 3: GOD, OUR INCREDIBLE CREATOR 9
  - CHAPTER 4: WHEN THINGS WENT WRONG: THE STORY OF SIN 13
  - CHAPTER 5: GOD'S AMAZING GRACE AND THE GREAT FLOOD: NOAH 17
- PART 2: GOD'S PROMISES IN THE OLD TESTAMENT 21
  - CHAPTER 6: GOD'S BIG PROMISE TO ABRAHAM 23
  - CHAPTER 7: GOD RESCUES HIS PEOPLE: MOSES AND THE EXODUS 28
  - CHAPTER 8: A SHEPHERD BOY BECOMES A KING: DAVID 33
- PART 3: THE GOOD NEWS OF JESUS 37
  - CHAPTER 9: GOD'S GREATEST GIFT: JESUS IS BORN! 39
  - CHAPTER 10: JESUS SHOWS US GOD'S LOVE 43
  - CHAPTER 11: JESUS SAVES US: THE CROSS AND THE EMPTY TOMB 47
- PART 4: LIVING FOR GOD 51
  - CHAPTER 12: TALKING WITH GOD: PRAYER AND HIS WORD 53
  - CHAPTER 13: GROWING IN FAITH: OBEYING, LOVING, AND SHARING 57
  - CHAPTER 14: YOUR FOREVER FRIEND: WALKING WITH JESUS 61
- CHECK OUT ANOTHER BOOK IN THE SERIES 66
- WELCOME ABOARD, CHECK OUT THIS LIMITED-TIME FREE BONUS! 67

Part 1: Discovering God's Truth in His Word

Chapter 1: Welcome to Your Bible Adventure!

Are you ready for an adventure that will take you through exciting stories, introduce you to incredible people, and help you discover the most important truths in the universe? That's what this book is all about.

This is your guide to understanding the Bible, which is **God's very own Word**. Think of it like a treasure map, and the treasure is knowing God better and growing stronger in your faith.

You might be wondering, "What is a Bible study, anyway?" It's simple: It means we're going to read parts of God's Word together, learn what they mean, and discover how God wants us to live because of what we learn. We'll explore big ideas in simple ways, and you'll find out how these stories are super important for your life today.

Here's how your adventure will work:
- **Bible Stories:** We'll read exciting stories straight from God's Word.
- **Simple Explanations:** We'll break down big ideas into easy-to-understand parts.
- **Big Lessons:** For each chapter, we'll find one main truth, a "Big Lesson," that God wants you to learn and remember.
- **Fun Activities:** You'll get to draw, write, think, and maybe even play some games. These activities will help you remember what you've learned.
- **Think & Grow:** We'll have questions and ideas to help you think about how God's truths apply to your own life.

This journey is all about growing closer to God. He loves you so much, and He wants you to know Him through His Word. So, open your heart and get ready.

Key Truth for Chapter 1: Learning about God from His Word helps us understand His amazing plan and grow closer to Him.

Activity Idea: Your Bible Adventure Passport

Let's get ready. Take a moment to think about what you hope to discover in this Bible study.
1. My Name: _____
2. Age: _____
3. One thing I already know about God's Word (the Bible):
   _____
4. One question I have about God or His Word:
   _____
5. One thing I hope to learn from this Bible study:
   _____

6. **My Bible Study Pledge:** (Put a checkmark next to each one you agree to.)
    - [ ] I will try my best to read and learn.
    - [ ] I will ask questions when I don't understand.
    - [ ] I will think about how God's Word can help me.
    - [ ] I will have fun learning about God.

Chapter 2: The Bible: God's Own Word

Have you ever wondered what the Bible actually *is*? It's **God's Own Word**. This means that even though human authors wrote down the words, God was working through them, making sure they wrote exactly what He wanted us to know. It's like when you tell a friend a message to write down. The words are yours, even if your friend does the writing.

The Bible is completely true and it's trustworthy.

Why is God's Word So Important?

1. **It Reveals God:** The Bible tells us *who God is*. It shows us His character: that He is loving, holy, just, powerful, and merciful.
2. **It Shows His Plan:** It explains God's plan for the world and for us, including His plan to rescue us from sin.
3. **It Teaches Us How to Live:** God's Word teaches us right from wrong and guides us on how to live in a way that pleases Him and blesses others. It's like an instruction manual for life.

How is God's Word Organized?

The Bible is a collection of 66 different books, but they all fit together perfectly. It's split into two main parts:

- **The Old Testament:** This part (39 books) tells us about God's creation of the world, how sin entered, God's promises, and His relationship with His chosen people, Israel, *before* Jesus came to earth. It talks about prophets, kings, wars, and miracles.
- **The New Testament:** This part (27 books) tells us all about Jesus: His birth, life, teachings, miracles, death, resurrection, and ascension. It also tells us how His followers spread the Good News and how Christians should live.

Each book in the Bible is divided into **chapters**, and each chapter is divided into smaller pieces called **verses**. This helps us find specific parts easily. For example, if someone says "Go to John 3:16," you know they mean the Book of John, Chapter 3, Verse 16.

So, when you open the Bible, you're not just reading ancient words. You're reading God's truth, His message to *you*.

Key Truth for Chapter 2: The Bible is God's inspired and unchanging Word, completely true and powerful, given to us so we can know Him.

Activity Idea: Bible Scavenger Hunt

Let's practice finding things in God's Word. Use a Bible (a physical one if you have it, or an online version) to find these verses. Write down what each verse talks about.

1. **Genesis 1:1:** (Hint: First verse of the Bible.) What does it say?

   _____

   _____

2. **John 3:16:** (Hint: A very famous verse about God's love.) What does it say?

   _____

   _____

3. **Psalm 23:1:** (Hint: A popular psalm about a shepherd.) What does it say?

   _____

   _____

4. **Matthew 28:19:** (Hint: Jesus' command to His followers.) What does it say?

   _____

   _____

Extra Challenge: Can you name two books from the Old Testament and two books from the New Testament?

Old Testament:
   1. _____
   2. _____

New Testament:
   1. _____
   2. _____

Chapter 3: God, Our Incredible Creator

Have you ever looked up at the stars at night? Or seen a tiny seed grow into a giant tree?

In the very first book of the Bible, Genesis, God's Word tells us the story about how everything began. It shows us that God made everything out of nothing, simply by speaking.

The Story of Creation (Genesis 1:1 - 2:3)

Imagine a time when there was nothing. No light, no land, no animals, no people, just darkness and water. Then, God's voice broke through the silence.

- **Day 1:** God said, "Let there be light," and light appeared. He separated the light from the darkness, calling the light "day" and the darkness "night."
- **Day 2:** God separated the waters below from the waters above, creating the sky.
- **Day 3:** God gathered the waters together to reveal dry land. He called the dry land "earth" and the gathered waters "seas." Then, He spoke, and the earth brought forth plants, trees, and all kinds of seeds and fruits.
- **Day 4:** God made the sun, moon, and stars to give light to the earth, to mark seasons, days, and years.
- **Day 5:** God filled the waters with swimming creatures and the sky with all kinds of birds. He blessed them and told them to multiply.
- **Day 6:** God commanded the earth to bring forth living creatures: livestock, creeping things, and wild animals, each according to its kind. And it was so.

But God wasn't finished. The most special part of creation happened on Day 6. **"Then God said, "Let us make mankind in our image, in our likeness, so that they may rule over the fish in the sea and the birds in the sky, over the livestock and all the wild animals, and over all the creatures that move along the ground."** (Genesis 1:26, NIV).

God created Adam and Eve in His own image. They were the first people on His Earth. He gave them the ability to think, choose, love, and care for His world. He wanted them to know and trust Him. He placed them in a beautiful garden called Eden and gave them the important job of taking care of His creation.

When God looked at everything He had made, He saw that "it was very good." (Genesis 1:31, NIV). On the seventh day, God rested from His work, setting an example for us. Now we take a day every week to rest and praise the Lord.

This story teaches us so much about God: He is all-powerful, wise, and good. He didn't *have* to create anything, but He did, out of His incredible love and goodness. And He made *you*.

You are wonderfully and purposefully made in the image of the great Creator God. He made you so that you can come to know Him. He gave you the freedom to choose love. He didn't program you like a robot, but gave you unlimited choices in life.

Key Truth for Chapter 3: God is the all-powerful and loving Creator of the universe, and He made us in His image, special and unique.

Activity Idea: Thank You, Creator God

Think about all the beautiful things God created. What are some of your favorites? Draw a picture in the space below of something God made that you are thankful for. Then, write a short prayer of thanks to God for being such an incredible Creator.

My Thank You Prayer to God: Dear God, Thank you for

_____

_____

Thank you for being my Creator and making me special. Amen.

Chapter 4: When Things Went Wrong: The Story of Sin

In our last chapter, we learned that God created everything perfectly and called it "very good." He made Adam and Eve to live in a beautiful garden called Eden, where they could enjoy His presence and the world He made. Everything was perfect.

Then, something terrible happened that changed everything.

The Story of the First Sin (Genesis 3:1-24)

God had given Adam and Eve only one rule: "And the Lord God commanded the man, "You are free to eat from any tree in the garden; but you must not eat from the tree of the knowledge of good and evil, for when you eat from it you will certainly die" (Genesis 2:16-17, NIV). This rule was for their protection and to remind them that God was in charge.

One day, the cunning serpent (who was actually Satan, God's enemy, in disguise) came to Eve. He twisted God's words and asked, "Did God really say, 'You must not eat from any tree in the garden'?" (Genesis 3:1, NIV)

Eve corrected him, explaining the one rule about the tree of the knowledge of good and evil.

The serpent lied, "You will not certainly die," the serpent said to the woman. "For God knows that when you eat from it your eyes will be opened, and you will be like God, knowing good and evil." (Genesis 3:4-5, NIV)

Eve listened to the lie instead of God's clear command. She took some fruit and ate it. Then she gave some to Adam, and he ate it too.

In that moment, Adam and Eve disobeyed God. This act of disobeying God is called **sin**. Sin is when we choose our own way instead of God's way.

Immediately, their eyes *were* opened, and they realized they were naked. They made coverings for themselves from fig leaves and hid from God when He came walking in the garden.

God called out to them. Adam admitted they had eaten the fruit. Instead of taking responsibility, Adam blamed Eve, and Eve blamed the serpent.

Sin always brings sad and serious consequences. God, who is perfectly holy and just, had to respond to their disobedience.

- The serpent was cursed to crawl on its belly.
- Eve would have pain in childbirth and struggle.
- Adam would have to work hard, and the ground would produce thorns and thistles.
- And most importantly, Adam and Eve could no longer stay in God's perfect garden.

So, the story of sin reminds us that disobeying God breaks our relationship with Him and causes pain. However, it also shows us that God never gives up on His plan to rescue us and bring us back to Himself.

Key Truth for Chapter 4: Sin separates us from our holy God, but God had a plan from the very beginning to save us and bring us back to Himself.

Activity Idea: Choices and Consequences Maze

Sometimes, one small choice can lead to big consequences. Trace the path through the maze below, thinking about how Adam and Eve's choice led to sadness.

Think & Grow:

1. What was the one rule God gave Adam and Eve?
_____
_____

2. What is sin? (Use your own words)
_____
_____

3. Even after Adam and Eve sinned, what promise did God give them?
_____
_____

4. Why is it important for us to obey God?
_____
_____

Chapter 5: God's Amazing Grace and the Great Flood: Noah

In our last chapter, we learned how sin entered the world through Adam and Eve, causing separation from God. Sadly, after that, sin spread very quickly among people. The Bible tells us in Genesis 6:5 that the Lord saw how great the wickedness of the human race had become on the earth, and that every inclination of the thoughts of the human heart was only evil all the time. God was heartbroken by how much people had turned away from Him.

Noah Finds Favor with God (Genesis 6)

God saw that people everywhere were doing wrong. Because God is just, He decided to judge the world.. He decided to bring a great flood to cleanse the earth. There was one person, however, who stood out. His name was Noah.

The Bible says, "But Noah found favor in the eyes of the Lord." (Genesis 6:8, NIV). Noah was a righteous man, blameless among the people of his time, and he walked faithfully with God.

God spoke to Noah and told him about the coming flood. He gave Noah very specific instructions to build a huge ark, or boat. This ark was not just any boat; it was enormous. God told Noah exactly how big it should be, what materials to use, and to build different rooms inside. God also told Noah to take animals into the ark with him, along with his wife, his three sons, and their wives. They would be saved from the flood.

This command to build an ark must have seemed very strange. There had probably never been a flood like this before, and Noah lived far from any large body of water. Noah did not question God. He simply obeyed everything God commanded him to do. He spent many, many years building the ark exactly as God instructed.

The Great Flood (Genesis 7-8)

When the ark was finished, Noah, his family, and all the animals went inside. Then, God Himself shut the door. It began to rain. It rained for forty days and forty nights. Water also burst up from the ground. The waters rose higher and higher until they covered the highest mountains on Earth. Every living thing on the dry land that breathed air died, except for those safely inside the ark.

The ark floated on the waters for many months. God remembered Noah and those with him in the ark. He sent a wind to blow over the earth, and the waters began to recede. After a long time, the ark came to rest on the mountains of Ararat. Noah sent out a raven, and then a dove, to see if the water had dried up. Finally, the dove returned with an olive leaf, showing that new life was appearing.

Noah, his family, and all the animals finally came out of the ark onto dry ground. Noah's first act was to build an altar to the Lord and offer sacrifices to Him, showing his thanks and worship.

God's Promise: The Rainbow Covenant (Genesis 9)

God was pleased with Noah's worship. God then made a special promise, a **covenant**, with Noah and all living creatures. God said, "I establish my covenant with you: Never again will all life be destroyed by the waters of a flood; never again will there be a flood to destroy the earth." (Genesis 9:11, NIV).

God gave a beautiful sign to remind everyone of this promise: the **rainbow!** Whenever we see a rainbow in the sky, it is a reminder of God's faithfulness and His promise never to destroy the earth again with a flood.

The story of Noah teaches us powerful truths about God. It shows us His perfect **justice** against sin and how seriously He takes disobedience. It also shows His **grace** and **mercy** by saving Noah and his family, and His unfailing **faithfulness** to keep His promises.

Key Truth for Chapter 5: God is just and hates sin, yet He is also merciful and faithful to those who obey Him, always keeping His promises.

Activity Idea: The Ark of Safety

Draw a picture of Noah's Ark on the water, with the animals going in or coming out, and a rainbow in the sky above it. Use bright colors for the rainbow.

Think & Grow:

1. Why did God decide to send the flood?
_____
_____

2. How was Noah different from most other people at that time?
_____
_____

3. What was the special sign God gave to remind us of His promise after the flood?
_____
_____

4. How does Noah's Ark help us understand Jesus?
_____
_____

Part 2: God's Promises in the Old Testament

Chapter 6: God's Big Promise to Abraham

After sin entered the world, humanity became more and more rebellious against God. People started to live in their own ways, not the way of God. In His perfect plan, He decided to start over with a special family, through whom He would bring blessings to the whole world. This is where a man named **Abram** comes into our story. God would later change his name to **Abraham**, meaning "father of many nations," as part of His great promise to him.

God's Call to Abram (Genesis 12:1-3)

Abram lived in a land far away, in a city called Ur. God spoke to him one day with an amazing command and promises. God told Abram, "Leave your country, your relatives, and your father's family, and go to the land I will show you."

God did not stop there. He then made incredible promises to Abram:

- "I will make you into a great nation."
- "I will bless you."
- "I will make your name great, and you will be a blessing."
- "I will bless those who bless you, and whoever curses you I will curse."
- "All peoples on earth will be blessed through you."

Think about that last promise. God was saying that through Abram's family, a blessing would come to *everyone* on Earth. This was a hint about Jesus, who would one day come from Abram's (now Abraham's) family line to save all people.

Abraham's Faith and Trust

Abraham faced a big decision. He had to leave everything he knew and go to a place God would only show him later. He had to trust God completely. Abraham did just that. He packed up his family, his belongings, and his nephew, Lot, and began the long journey, following God's leading. Abraham chose to believe God's promises, even though he could not see how they would happen.

Years passed, and Abraham and his wife, Sarah (who used to be called Sarai), grew very old. They still did not have any children. God had promised Abraham many descendants, as many as the stars in the sky.

Abraham might have wondered how this could ever happen. He kept trusting God. The Bible tells us that because Abraham believed the Lord, God counted it to him as righteousness. This means God declared Abraham right and good in His sight because of his faith.

God Keeps His Promises

Finally, when Abraham was 100 years old and Sarah was 90, God miraculously kept His promise. Sarah gave birth to a son, and they named him Isaac, which means "he laughs".

Later, God tested Abraham's faith in the most difficult way (Genesis 22). God told Abraham to take Isaac, his only son, to Moriah and offer him as a sacrifice. This must have been heartbreaking for Abraham. He loved Isaac deeply, and Isaac was the child through whom all of God's promises were supposed to continue.

Abraham obeyed, trusting God's wisdom and goodness. As Abraham was about to offer Isaac, an angel of the Lord called out, stopping him. God saw Abraham's faith and provided a ram caught in a thicket to be sacrificed instead.

Because of Abraham's obedience and faith, God again blessed him, "I will surely bless you and make your descendants as numerous as the stars in the sky and as the sand on the seashore. Your descendants will take possession of the cities of their enemies, and through your offspring all nations on earth will be blessed, because you have obeyed me." (Genesis 22:17-18, NIV)

This story teaches us that God is always faithful. He rewarded Abraham's faith, and through Abraham's family, God prepared the way for the greatest blessing of all: Jesus.

Key Truth for Chapter 5: God is faithful and always keeps His promises, even when we don't understand how.

Activity Idea: Promise Path

Draw a winding path starting from "Abram's Home (Ur)" and ending at "God's Promise Kept (Isaac's Birth)." Along the path, write or draw symbols for the different promises God made to Abram/Abraham and moments where he showed faith.

Think & Grow:

1. What was one big promise God made to Abram (Abraham)?

_____

_____

2. How did Abraham show that he trusted God?

_____

_____

3. Why is it important for us to trust God's promises today?

_____

_____

4. Can you think of a time when God kept a promise to you or someone you know?

_____

_____

Chapter 7: God Rescues His People: Moses and the Exodus

Remember how God promised Abraham that his descendants would become a great nation? Years later, Abraham's family had grown into a huge group of people called the Israelites. They had moved to Egypt, a powerful country. A new Pharaoh came to power there, and he became afraid of the Israelites' growing numbers. He forced them into cruel slavery, making their lives incredibly hard.

Moses: A Baby in a Basket (Exodus 1-2)

Pharaoh became so fearful of the Israelites that he gave a terrible command: every baby boy born to an Israelite family had to be thrown into the Nile River. It was a horrible way the Pharaoh wanted to use to ensure the babies would not survive. This was a very dark time for God's people.

An Israelite mother, however, gave birth to a beautiful baby boy. She hid him for three months, keeping him safe. When she could no longer hide him, she bravely put him in a basket and placed it among the reeds along the bank of the Nile River, trusting God for his safety. Moses's older sister, Miriam, watched from a distance to see what would happen.

Pharaoh's own daughter came down to the river to bathe. She saw the basket among the reeds and sent her servant girl to get it. When she opened the basket, she saw the baby boy crying. Her heart was filled with pity for him. She knew he was one of the Hebrew (Israelite) babies.

Miriam then stepped forward and bravely asked Pharaoh's daughter, "Shall I go and get one of the Hebrew women to nurse the baby for you?" Pharaoh's daughter agreed. Miriam quickly went and brought the baby's own mother. Pharaoh's daughter told the mother to nurse the baby for her, and she would even pay her.

So, this little baby, who was later named Moses (which means "drawn out," because he was drawn out of the water), grew up in Pharaoh's palace as if he were Pharaoh's own grandson. God had a special plan for Moses, saving him from death and preparing him to lead His people.

God Calls Moses (Exodus 3)

Years later, Moses saw an Egyptian mistreating an Israelite. He acted quickly, killing the Egyptian. Pharaoh found out, and Moses had to flee Egypt to save his life. He lived as a shepherd for many years in a faraway land. One day, God appeared to Moses in a burning bush that was not burned up. God told Moses that He had seen the suffering of His people and planned to rescue them. God sent Moses back to Pharaoh to demand freedom for the Israelites. Moses felt scared and unsure, but God promised to be with him and give him the power he needed.

God's Mighty Power: The Plagues

Moses and his brother Aaron went to Pharaoh. They told him, "This is what the Lord, the God of Israel, says: 'Let My people go!'" Pharaoh refused to listen. He made the Israelites work even harder.

God then sent ten powerful plagues upon Egypt to show Pharaoh, and the whole world, that He alone is the true God. These were not random disasters. Each plague showed that the false gods of Egypt had no power. Each plague attacked something the Egyptians worshipped or a part of their daily life.

- The Nile River turned to blood.
- Frogs, gnats, and flies swarmed the land.
- Their livestock died.
- Painful boils covered the people.
- Hail destroyed crops.
- Locusts ate everything remaining.
- A thick darkness covered Egypt for three days.

Pharaoh remained stubborn through most of the plagues. Each time he promised to let the Israelites go, then changed his mind.

The Passover: God's Protection (Exodus 12)

The tenth and final plague was the most serious. God declared He would send an angel to strike down the firstborn son in every Egyptian home. God provided a way for His people, the Israelites, to be saved. He commanded each Israelite family to sacrifice a perfect lamb and put some of its blood on the doorposts of their homes. When the death angel passed through Egypt, he would "pass over" any house marked with the lamb's blood.

This was a powerful picture. This event is called the **Passover**. It points us directly to Jesus, who is the Lamb of God. Just like the blood of the lamb protected Israel, Jesus saved us by giving His life for us. He was the ultimate sacrifice, and he did it for you.

Freedom Through the Red Sea (Exodus 14)

After the terrifying final plague, Pharaoh finally told the Israelites to leave. They rushed out of Egypt, free at last. Pharaoh quickly changed his mind again. He gathered his mighty army and chased after them. The Israelites found themselves trapped between Pharaoh's army and the vast Red Sea.

They were terrified, but God had a plan. Moses stretched out his staff over the sea, and God miraculously parted the waters. The Israelites walked across on dry ground, with walls of water on both sides. As Pharaoh's army tried to follow, God brought the waters crashing down, destroying the Egyptian army. God had powerfully delivered His people.

God Gives His Law: The Ten Commandments (Exodus 20)

God led the Israelites through the wilderness to Mount Sinai. There, God spoke directly to His people, giving them His holy laws, known as the **Ten Commandments**. These commandments were not given so people could earn their way into heaven. God had already rescued them by His grace. The laws were given to teach them how to live as His holy people, how to love Him, and how to love each other.

This journey from slavery to freedom, and receiving God's laws, showed Israel that God is mighty to save, trustworthy, and holy. He always keeps His covenant to   His people. A covenant is an unbreakable bond and commitment that lasts forever.

Key Truth for Chapter 6: God powerfully delivers His people from trouble and gives us His holy law to guide us because He loves us and desires our good.

Activity Idea: Decode the Ten Commandments

God gave us these good rules to help us live. Here are some of the Ten Commandments in simpler words. Can you match the command to what it teaches us?

Commands (Mix & Match):

1. You shall have no other gods before Me.
2. You shall not misuse the name of the Lord your God.
3. Remember the Sabbath day by keeping it holy.
4. Honor your father and your mother.
5. You shall not murder.
6. You shall not commit adultery.
7. You shall not steal.
8. You shall not give false testimony against your neighbor.
9. You shall not covet your neighbor's house.
10. You shall not make for yourself an idol.

What it Teaches Us (Match with the numbers above):

- _____ Don't want what belongs to others.
- _____ Show respect to your parents.
- _____ Worship only the one true God.
- _____ Do not take what is not yours.
- _____ Do not say bad or disrespectful things about God.
- _____ Keep special time for God to rest and worship.
- _____ Don't harm or take someone's life.
- _____ Be faithful in marriage (for grown-ups).
- _____ Don't worship statues or false gods.
- _____ Do not lie about someone.

Connect the Dots: Passover and Jesus

Draw a line from the "Passover Lamb" to "Jesus" and write one sentence about how the Passover helps us understand what Jesus did for us.

[Draw a picture of a lamb and a cross with space for text]

Chapter 8: A Shepherd Boy Becomes a King: David

God had established Israel as a nation and given them His laws. The people eventually asked for a king, just like the other nations. God chose a tall, strong man named Saul to be their first king. King Saul disobeyed God, however, leading God to choose a new king. God told the prophet Samuel to go to Bethlehem to the house of Jesse, for one of Jesse's sons would be the next king.

God Chooses a King After His Own Heart (1 Samuel 16)

Samuel saw Jesse's strong, handsome sons, one by one. Each time, God told Samuel, "Do not consider his appearance or his height, for I have rejected him. The Lord does not look at the things people look at. People look at the outward appearance, but the Lord looks at the heart." (1 Samuel 16:7, NIV).

Finally, Jesse sent for his youngest son, David. David was just a boy, a shepherd. As soon as Samuel saw him, God said, "This is the one; anoint him." Samuel poured olive oil on David's head, showing that God had chosen him to be the next king. From that day on, the Spirit of the Lord came powerfully upon David.

David and the Giant Goliath (1 Samuel 17)

A terrible problem arose for Israel. Their enemy, the Philistines, had gathered for war. Their champion was a giant warrior named Goliath. He wore heavy armor and carried a huge spear. Goliath came out every day and challenged the Israelite army: "Send out a man to fight me! If he wins, we will be your slaves. If I win, you will be our slaves!"

The Israelites were terrified. King Saul himself was afraid.

And Goliath taunted the Israelites for forty days.

Young David arrived at the battlefield, bringing food for his older brothers. He heard Goliath's challenge and saw the fear in the Israelite army. David felt angry that this giant was defying the armies of the living God.

He bravely told King Saul he would fight Goliath. Saul tried to give David his own heavy armor, but it was too big. David knew he did not need heavy armor or a sword. He went to a stream, picked up five smooth stones, and took his shepherd's sling.

David faced the giant, saying, "You come against me with sword and spear and javelin, but I come against you in the name of the Lord Almighty, the God of the armies of Israel, whom you have defied. This day the Lord will deliver you into my hands, and I'll strike you down and cut off your head. This very day I will give the carcasses of the Philistine army to the birds and the wild animals, and the whole world will know that there is a God in Israel." (1 Samuel 17:45-46, NIV).

David put a stone in his sling, swung it, and hit Goliath squarely in the forehead. The giant fell to the ground! David then ran and cut off Goliath's head. The Philistines saw their champion was dead and fled in terror. God gave the victory to Israel through a courageous shepherd boy who trusted Him. David became a national hero and eventually, Israel's beloved king.

David's Sin and God's Forgiveness (2 Samuel 11-12, Psalm 51)

King David was a great king, leading Israel and worshipping God. He was known as a "man after God's own heart." Even good people, however, can make bad choices. One day, David stayed home from battle.

He saw a woman named Bathsheba, and he sinned by taking her to be with him, even though she was married. David then arranged for her husband, Uriah, a loyal soldier, to be killed in battle to cover up his sin.

God sent the prophet Nathan to confront David with his sin. Nathan told David a story about a rich man who stole a poor man's only lamb. David became very angry, saying the rich man deserved to die. Nathan then pointed at David and said, "You are the man!"

David immediately recognized his sin. He was heartbroken and truly sorry. He cried out to God in repentance, saying, "I have sinned against the Lord." He later wrote Psalm 51, a prayer asking for God's forgiveness and a clean heart.

God is holy and just, so David's sin had serious consequences for his family and kingdom. God is also merciful and forgiving. Because David genuinely confessed his sin and turned back to God, God forgave him. This shows us that God will always forgive us when we truly confess our sins and turn away from them. Even though we mess up, God is ready to offer His grace and a new start.

Key Truth for Chapter 7: God sees our hearts, uses even our weaknesses for His glory, and graciously forgives us when we turn back to Him.

Activity Idea: Heart Check

Remember what God told Samuel: "People look at the outward appearance, but the Lord looks at the heart."

1. What are some "outward appearances" people might see about you? (e.g., your clothes, your hair, how tall you are, if you're good at sports).

_____
_____
_____

2. What are some things God sees in your heart? (e.g., your thoughts, your feelings, if you love Him, if you try to obey Him, if you're kind).

_____
_____
_____

Part 3: The Good News of Jesus

Chapter 9: God's Greatest Gift: Jesus is Born!

We have explored many incredible stories from the Old Testament: Creation, the spread of sin, God's justice in the flood, His promise to Abraham, His mighty rescue of Israel through Moses, and His faithfulness to David.

All these stories, in different ways, were pointing to something even greater to come. They were like hints or puzzle pieces waiting for the final, most important piece.

God Sends His Son (Matthew 1:18-25, Luke 2:1-20)

Hundreds of years after David, God would send His promised Savior. This Savior would be unlike any other. He would be God's own Son, born into the world.

God chose a young woman named Mary to be the mother of this special child. Mary was a virgin, meaning she had never been married or had children. She was betrothed to marry Joseph, who would become her husband.

An angel named Gabriel appeared to her and told her she would have a baby boy through the power of the Holy Spirit.

An angel also appeared to Joseph in a dream with the following message: "Joseph son of David, do not be afraid to take Mary home as your wife, because what is conceived in her is from the Holy Spirit. She will give birth to a son, and you are to give him the name Jesus, because he will save his people from their sins (Matthew 1:20-21, NIV).

A special decree from the Roman Emperor Caesar Augustus made everyone travel to their hometowns to be counted for taxes. Joseph and Mary, who was very pregnant, had to travel a long way from Nazareth to Bethlehem, the town of David. When they arrived, the town was so crowded that there was no room for them anywhere, not even at the inn. They had to stay in a stable, a place where animals lived.

While they were there, Mary's baby was born. She wrapped her baby, Jesus, in cloths and laid Him gently in a manger, which was a feeding trough for animals.

On a hillside nearby, shepherds were watching their sheep. Suddenly, an angel of the Lord appeared to them, and the glory of the Lord shone around them. The shepherds were terrified. The angel told them, "Do not be afraid. I bring you good news that will cause great joy for all the people. Today in the town of David a Savior has been born to you; he is the Messiah, the Lord." (Luke 2:10-11, NIV). The angel explained they would find the baby wrapped in cloths and lying in a manger.

Suddenly, a huge crowd of angels appeared, praising God and saying, "Glory to God in the highest heaven, and on earth peace to those on whom His favor rests!"

The shepherds quickly went to Bethlehem and found Mary, Joseph, and the baby Jesus, just as the angel had told them. They told everyone what they had seen and heard. Everyone who heard their story was amazed.

Wise Men Worship the King (Matthew 2:1-12)

News of this special King spread far and wide. Wise men from the East, who studied the stars, saw a unique star that indicated the King of the Jews had been born. They traveled a long distance, following this star, all the way to Jerusalem. There, they began asking, "Where is the one who has been born king of the Jews? We saw His star when it rose and have come to worship Him."

King Herod, the current ruler, heard this and became very troubled. He secretly called the wise men and found out from them the exact time the star had appeared. He then sent them to Bethlehem, saying, "Go and search carefully for the child. As soon as you find him, report to me, so that I too may go and worship him." (Matthew 2:7, NIV)

The wise men continued to Bethlehem, guided by the star, which stopped over the place where the child was. They were filled with joy.

They bowed down and worshipped Him, offering Him precious gifts: gold (fit for a king), frankincense (a special incense used in worship, fit for God), and myrrh (a spice used for burial).

After their visit, God warned the wise men in a dream not to return to Herod, so they went back to their country by another route.

Jesus' birth was the moment God's biggest promise began to truly unfold. It was the beginning of God's rescue plan for all humanity. Jesus came to earth to teach us about God, and to make a way for us to be forgiven of our sins and have a relationship with God forever.

Key Truth for Chapter 9: Jesus is God's promised Savior, sent to earth as a baby to rescue us from sin and bring us eternal life.

Activity Idea: Prophecy Connection

The Old Testament gave many hints (prophecies) about where and how Jesus would be born. Draw a line to connect the Old Testament prophecy to its New Testament fulfillment in Jesus' birth.

Old Testament Prophecy:
1. Born in Bethlehem (Micah 5:2)
2. Born of a virgin (Isaiah 7:14)
3. Called "God with us" (Isaiah 7:14)**New Testament Fulfillment (Jesus' Birth):**

- [ ] Joseph was told to name him Immanuel, which means "God with us" (Matthew 1:23).
- [ ] Mary, a virgin, became pregnant by the Holy Spirit (Luke 1:34-35).
- [ ] Jesus was born in Bethlehem, as Joseph and Mary traveled there (Luke 2:4-7).

Draw the Nativity Scene

Use the space below to draw your own picture of the Nativity, showing Baby Jesus in the manger, Mary and Joseph, and perhaps some shepherds or angels.

Chapter 10: Jesus Shows Us God's Love

Jesus grew up in the town of Nazareth. He learned and became strong, filled with wisdom. God's favor was on Him (Luke 2:52). When He was about 30 years old, Jesus began His special work, called His ministry.

For about three years, Jesus traveled around, teaching people about God's Kingdom and showing them who God truly is. He did two main things: He performed miracles, and He taught powerful lessons. Both showed us God's incredible love and power.

Jesus Heals and Forgives: The Paralyzed Man (Mark 2:1-12)

One day, Jesus was teaching in a house in Capernaum. So many people crowded around the door that there was no room left, not even outside. Four men carried their friend, who could not walk on a mat. They desperately wanted Jesus to heal him. They could not get through the crowd.

The men did not give up. They had an idea. They carried their friend to the roof of the house. They carefully dug a hole through the roof above where Jesus was teaching. Then, they gently lowered their friend on his mat right down in front of Jesus.

Jesus saw their great faith. He did not immediately say, "Get up and walk!" Instead, He looked at the paralyzed man and said, "Son, your sins are forgiven."

Some religious teachers sitting there thought, "Who can forgive sins? Only God can do that!" Jesus knew what they were thinking. He said to them, "Which is easier: to say to this paralyzed man, 'Your sins are forgiven,' or to say, 'Get up, take your mat and walk'?"

Jesus then told them, "I want you to know that the Son of Man has authority on earth to forgive sins." He turned to the man and commanded, "I tell you, get up, take your mat and go home."

Immediately, the man stood up, took his mat, and walked out right in front of everyone! The crowd was amazed and praised God, saying, "We have never seen anything like this!" This miracle showed Jesus' power over sickness and, even more importantly, His divine power to forgive sins.

Jesus Teaches About God's Love: The Lost Son (Luke 15:11-32)

Jesus also taught people through stories called **parables**. Parables are like earthly stories with heavenly meanings. They help us understand big truths about God's Kingdom. Here is one of His most famous parables:

Jesus told a story about a man who had two sons. The younger son told his father, "Father, give me my share of the inheritance." This was a very disrespectful thing to ask, as it meant he wished his father were already dead! The loving father, however, divided his property between his two sons.

The younger son quickly gathered all his money and traveled to a faraway country. There, he wasted all his money on foolish and wild living. A terrible famine (a time when there was no food) came to that land, and the young man became very poor. He was so desperate that he got a job feeding pigs, which was a very shameful job for a Jewish person. He was so hungry, he even wanted to eat the pods the pigs were eating.

Finally, he came to his senses. He thought, "My father's hired servants have more than enough food, and here I am starving to death! I will go back to my father and say to him, 'Father, I have sinned against heaven and against you. I am no longer worthy to be called your son; make me like one of your hired servants.'"

He started his long journey home. While he was still a long way off, his father saw him. The father's heart was filled with compassion! He ran to his son, threw his arms around him, and kissed him.

The son started his prepared speech, "Father, I have sinned against heaven and against you. I am no longer worthy..." The father did not let him finish. He immediately told his servants, "Quick! Bring the best robe and put it on him. Put a ring on his finger and sandals on his feet. Bring the fattened calf and kill it. Let's have a feast and celebrate. This son of mine was dead and is alive again; he was lost and is found!" And so, they began to celebrate.

Meanwhile, the older brother was in the field working. As he approached the house, he heard music and dancing. He became angry when he learned his wasteful brother was being celebrated. His father went out to plead with him, explaining, "My son, you are always with me, and everything I have is yours. We had to celebrate and be glad, because this brother of yours was dead and is alive again; he was lost and found."

This parable teaches us about God's incredible love and forgiveness. The father represents God, and the lost son represents anyone who turns away from God through sin. God is always watching, waiting, and ready to welcome us home with open arms when we turn from our wrong ways and come back to Him. He celebrates when we return.

Both Jesus' powerful miracles and His loving teachings perfectly show us who God is. He is full of power, wisdom, and an endless supply of love for us.

Key Truth for Chapter 10: Jesus is God incarnate, perfectly demonstrating God's power, love, and truth through His life and teachings.

Activity Idea: Parable Power

The Parable of the Lost Son teaches us that God is ready to forgive.
What did the younger son do that was wrong?
_____
_____

How did the father show he loved his son, even when the son had messed up?
_____
_____

What does this parable teach you about how God feels when we mess up and then turn back to Him?
_____
_____

Show God's Love

Think of some ways Jesus showed love to people in the stories you know (healing, teaching, forgiving). List two ways here:
_____
_____
_____
_____

Now, think of one way *you* can show God's love to someone this week. My plan:

Chapter 11: Jesus Saves Us: The Cross and the Empty Tomb

We have seen how Jesus came to earth, born as a baby, and how He showed God's love through His powerful miracles and wise teachings. Every miracle and every parable pointed to one big reason why Jesus came: to rescue us from our sins and bring us back to God. This rescue mission required the greatest act of love and sacrifice ever known.

The Cross: Jesus' Sacrifice for Sin (Matthew 27)

Religious leaders in Jerusalem felt jealous of Jesus and did not believe He was the Son of God. They arrested Him and put Him on an unfair trial. People shouted for Him to be crucified, a very painful way of dying that was common at that time.

Jesus, though innocent, allowed Himself to be nailed to a cross. He suffered terribly there. He was not just suffering physical pain; He was taking the punishment for every wrong thing you and I have ever done, or will ever do. He carried the weight of the world's sin. As He hung on the cross, the sky became dark for three hours. Jesus cried out, "It is finished!" and then He died. He gave His life willingly, out of unimaginable love for us.

Jesus' body was taken down from the cross and placed in a tomb, a cave-like grave, cut out of rock. A large stone was rolled in front of the entrance, and guards were placed there to make sure no one could steal His body. It seemed like the story had ended in sadness.

The Empty Tomb: Jesus Conquers Death (Matthew 28, Luke 24)

A miraculous event took place on the third day after Jesus' death. Early on Sunday morning, some women who loved Jesus went to the tomb to prepare His body. They wondered who would roll away the heavy stone for them. As they arrived, they saw that the stone had already been rolled away.

An angel of the Lord sat on top of it. His clothes were white as snow. The guards were so terrified they fainted.

The angel told the women, "Do not be afraid, for I know that you are looking for Jesus, who was crucified. He is not here; He has risen, just as He said!" The angel invited them to see the empty place where Jesus' body had been. The women ran quickly to tell Jesus' disciples the Good News.

Jesus had truly risen from the dead. This proved that He is indeed the Son of God. It showed He had complete power over sin, death, and even the grave itself. Over the next 40 days, Jesus appeared to His disciples and many other people, showing them He was alive. He taught them more about God's Kingdom.

The Ascension: Jesus Returns to Heaven (Acts 1:6-11)

Forty days after His resurrection, Jesus gathered His disciples on a mountain. He gave them a final instruction to go into all the world and share the Good News about Him. Then, as they watched, Jesus was lifted up into the sky. A cloud took Him out of their sight. Two angels stood nearby and told the disciples that Jesus would return in the same way He left.

Jesus is now in heaven, sitting at the right hand of God the Father. He is reigning as King, and He is preparing a place for all who believe in Him. His ascension means He is powerfully ruling and will one day return to gather His people and make all things new.

Jesus' death, resurrection, and ascension are the most important events in history. His death paid the penalty for our sins. His resurrection means He conquered death and offers us new, eternal life. His ascension means He is our reigning King who will come back for us. This is the amazing Good News of Jesus.

Key Truth for Chapter 11: Jesus died on the cross to pay the penalty for our sins and rose again, defeating death, so that all who believe in Him can have forgiveness and eternal life with God.

Activity Idea: The Empty Tomb

Draw a picture of the empty tomb on Easter morning. You can include the stone rolled away, angels, or the amazed women. What do you think it felt like to see that empty tomb?

What Does It Mean for You?

Jesus died and rose again for *you*!

1. Because Jesus died on the cross, what can you receive?

_____

_____

2. Because Jesus rose from the dead, what hope do you have?

_____

_____

Part 4: Living for God

Chapter 12: Talking with God: Prayer and His Word

We have learned that God created us, that sin separated us from Him, and that Jesus came to rescue us by dying for our sins and rising again. Now that Jesus has made a way for us to have a relationship with God, how do we actually *do* that?

It is like any friendship. You build a friendship by spending time together, talking, and listening. Our relationship with God works the same way. We talk to God through **prayer**, and we listen to God when we read His **Word**, the Bible.

Talking to God: Prayer

What is prayer? Prayer is simply talking to God. He is always ready and willing to listen to you, no matter where you are or what time it is. You do not need special words or to be in a special place. You can talk to Him in your heart, out loud, kneeling, standing, or even running.

What can you pray about? Anything!

- **Thank Him:** Thank God for His love, for Jesus, for your family, for nature, for food, for anything good in your life. (Psalm 107:1)
- **Tell Him Your Worries:** Share your fears, your struggles, or anything that makes you sad or anxious. God cares about everything that concerns you. (Philippians 4:6)
- **Ask for Help:** Ask God for wisdom when you need to make a choice, for strength when you are weak, or for help for yourself and others. (Matthew 7:7)
- **Say Sorry:** When you mess up or sin, you can tell God you are sorry, just like David did. He promises to forgive you. (1 John 1:9)
- **Pray for Others:** Ask God to help your family, friends, teachers, or anyone you know who needs Him. This is called interceding. (1 Timothy 2:1)

God is never too busy to hear you. He loves it when His children talk to Him.

Listening to God: His Word (The Bible)

God wants to talk to us too! He speaks to us through His inspired Word, the Bible. The Bible is not just an old book; it is God's living message to you.

Why should you read the Bible?

- **To Know God:** The Bible is how we learn about God's character, His plans, His love, and His power.
- **To Know His Will:** It teaches us how God wants us to live, what pleases Him, and what helps us make good choices.

- **To Get Wisdom:** It gives us guidance, comfort, and strength for every situation in life. (Psalm 119:105)
- **To Grow in Faith:** The more you read about God, the more you will trust Him and grow closer to Him.

How can you read the Bible? You do not have to read a whole book at once. You can start with a few verses each day. Maybe begin with a book like John in the New Testament to learn more about Jesus, or the Psalms for powerful prayers, or Proverbs for wise advice. You can also ask your parents or a trusted adult to help you find good parts to read. When you read, ask the Holy Spirit to help you understand what God wants you to learn.

Building a Relationship with God

Prayer and reading God's Word work together like two sides of a conversation. You talk to God, and God talks to you. When you do both regularly, your relationship with God will grow stronger and stronger. He wants to know you personally, and He wants you to know Him deeply.

Key Truth for Chapter 12: God desires a personal relationship with us, and we build this relationship by talking to Him in prayer and listening to Him through His Word.

Activity Idea: My Prayer & Bible Bites Journal

It is a great idea to keep track of your prayers and what you learn from God's Word. Here is a simple journal template you can use:

My Prayer & Bible Bites Journal

Date:

My Prayer to God (What I want to talk to Him about):

_____
_____
_____
_____

Bible Bite! (What I read today):

Book: _____
Chapter: _____
Verse(s): _____

What I learned from God's Word today:

_____

_____

How I can apply this to my life:

_____

_____

My Favorite Bible Verse Drawing:

Choose one Bible verse you really like. Write it out here, and then draw a picture that helps you remember it.

My Favorite Verse:

_____

_____

_____

Chapter 13: Growing in Faith: Obeying, Loving, and Sharing

You have learned so much in this Bible adventure. You know that God is our Creator, that sin separated us from Him, and that Jesus came to rescue us. You also know that you can talk to God and listen to Him through His Word. This is how we begin to know God. What happens next? We start to grow in our faith.

Growing in faith means becoming more and more like Jesus. It is not just about knowing *about* God in your head; it is about living *for* God with your whole heart, every single day. The Holy Spirit, who lives in everyone who trusts Jesus, helps us do this. The Holy Spirit gives us power and guidance to grow in three important ways: by obeying God, by loving others, and by sharing the Good News of Jesus.

1. Obeying God's Word

Why should we obey God? We obey God not to earn His love or get to heaven. We obey God because we *love* Him and want to please Him. It shows our thankfulness for His gift of salvation.

God's commands, like the Ten Commandments and all of Jesus' teachings, are always good. They are like instructions from a loving Parent who knows what is best for us. Obeying God keeps us safe, helps us live wisely, and brings joy. The Holy Spirit gives us the strength to choose what is right, even when it is hard.

2. Loving Others

Jesus gave us a very clear command: "Jesus replied: "'Love the Lord your God with all your heart and with all your soul and with all your mind.' This is the first and greatest commandment. And the second is like it: 'Love your neighbor as yourself." (Matthew 22:37-39, NIV). God showed us the greatest love by sending Jesus. We can show our love for God by loving the people around us.

How can you show love to others?

- **Be kind:** Use kind words, offer a helping hand, or give a cheerful smile.
- **Forgive others:** Everyone makes mistakes. Choose to forgive those who hurt you, just as God forgives you.
- **Share:** Share your toys, snacks, or even your time with someone who needs it.
- **Be patient:** Show patience with your family and friends, even when things get difficult.
- **Listen:** Really listen when someone is talking to you.
- **Help out:** Do chores without being asked, or offer to help someone with a task.

When you love others, you are showing them God's love, and that is a beautiful thing.

3. Sharing the Good News

Imagine you found the best news ever, maybe a secret map to a treasure or a cure for all sickness. Would you keep it to yourself? Of course not! You would want to share it with everyone.

The Good News about Jesus is the best news in the whole world! Everyone needs to hear that God loves them, that Jesus died for their sins, and that they can have eternal life with Him. You can be a part of sharing this news.

How can you share the Good News?

- **Live by example:** Let people see Jesus in you through your kindness, joy, and peace.
- **Tell your story:** Share what God has done for you and how Jesus has changed your life. You do not need to know everything; just share what you know.
- **Invite a friend:** Invite a friend to Sunday school, church, or a Christian club where they can learn more about Jesus.
- **Answer questions:** If someone asks you about your faith, try to answer honestly and gently.

Sharing Jesus does not have to be scary. You are simply telling people about the greatest friend you have.

Growing in faith is a lifelong journey. You will keep learning and changing as you follow Jesus. God is with you every step of the way, helping you to obey, to love, and to share His incredible Good News.

Key Truth for Chapter 13: When we trust Jesus, the Holy Spirit helps us grow more like Him, so we can obey God, love others, and share His Good News with the world.

Activity Idea: Love in Action Checklist

How can you show God's love this week? Check off the boxes as you do these things, or write in your own ideas!

- [ ] Help a parent or guardian with a chore without being asked.
- [ ] Say a kind word to someone who looks sad.
- [ ] Share something (a toy, a snack, a drawing) with a sibling or friend.

- [ ] Forgive someone who upset you.
- [ ] Listen carefully when someone is talking.
- [ ] Pray for a friend or family member.
- [ ] **My own idea:** _____
- [ ] **My own idea:** _____

Sharing Jesus with the World

Draw a picture of yourself sharing the Good News of Jesus. This could be you talking, being kind,

Chapter 14: Your Forever Friend: Walking with Jesus

Wow! You have come so far on this Bible adventure. You have learned about God's creation, how sin messed things up, and God's incredible plan to send Jesus to rescue us. You know how to talk to God through prayer and listen to Him through His Word. You also understand how to grow in your faith by obeying, loving, and sharing.

Now, it is important to remember that this is the beginning of a great journey. Your relationship with God, through Jesus, is a forever journey. Jesus is not just a historical figure or a powerful Savior. He is your **Forever Friend**.

Jesus: Always with You

Think about your best friend. You love spending time with them, talking to them, and doing things together. Jesus wants that kind of relationship with you, only even deeper and more special.

- **He is always with you:** Jesus promised His disciples, "I am with you always, to the very end of the age." (Matthew 28:20). He is with you when you are happy, when you are sad, when you are playing, and when you are trying to sleep. You are never alone.

- **He understands you:** Jesus lived as a human being. He experienced hunger, tiredness, joy, and even sadness. He understands your feelings and what you go through. (Hebrews 4:15).

- **He guides you:** Jesus wants to help you make good choices and live a life that honors God. He will guide you through His Holy Spirit, through His Word, and sometimes even through wise people around you. (Psalm 32:8).

- **He helps you:** When you face difficult things, or when you feel weak, Jesus gives you strength. You can do all things through Him who gives you strength. (Philippians 4:13).

- **He loves you unconditionally:** There is nothing you can do to make Jesus love you more, and nothing you can do to make Him love you less. His love is perfect and never fails. (Romans 8:38-39).

The Journey Continues

Walking with Jesus is an ongoing adventure. You will keep learning new things about God every day. You will face new challenges, however, you will also experience new joys.

Keep doing the things you have learned in this book:

- Keep talking to God in prayer.
- Keep reading His Word, the Bible.

- Keep choosing to obey Him in the big and small things.
- Keep loving others with His love.
- Keep sharing the Good News about Jesus with your words and actions.

You will fall down sometimes, everyone does. A forgiving God is always ready to pick you up and help you try again. He is patient and kind.

Your Forever Hope: Heaven and Jesus' Return

The best part of walking with Jesus is the incredible hope we have for the future. Jesus went to heaven after He rose from the dead. He is not just "gone"; He is there right now, preparing a place for all who believe in Him. He said, "And if I go and prepare a place for you, I will come back and take you to be with me that you also may be where I am." (John 14:3, NIV).

One day, Jesus will return to earth. He will come back for His people, and we will be with Him forever in heaven. There will be no more sadness, no more pain, only perfect joy and perfect peace in God's presence.

So, trust Jesus with your whole heart. Lean on Him. Talk to Him. Listen to Him. Enjoy every step of this incredible, forever adventure with your best friend, Jesus.

Key Truth for Chapter 14: Jesus is always with you as your forever friend, and He promises to guide you, help you, and welcome you into His eternal presence one day.

Activity Idea: My Promise from God

The Bible is full of God's promises to us. Find one of these verses (or another one you love) and write it out. This promise is for YOU.

- "I am with you always, to the very end of the age." (Matthew 28:20)
- "I can do all this through Him who gives me strength." (Philippians 4:13)
- "For God so loved the world that He gave His one and only Son, that whoever believes in Him shall not perish but have eternal life." (John 3:16)

My Favorite Promise:

Drawing My Future with Jesus

What do you imagine it will be like to be with Jesus in heaven forever? Draw a picture of what you think it might look like, or draw yourself walking with Jesus now.

My Commitment Prayer:

You have reached the end of this book, but just the beginning of your journey with Jesus. You can pray this simple prayer:

Dear Jesus, Thank you for being my Forever Friend. Thank you for loving me, dying for my sins, and rising again. I want to walk with You every day. Please guide me, help me to obey You, and show me how to love others and share Your Good News. I look forward to being with You forever. Amen.

Check out another book in the series

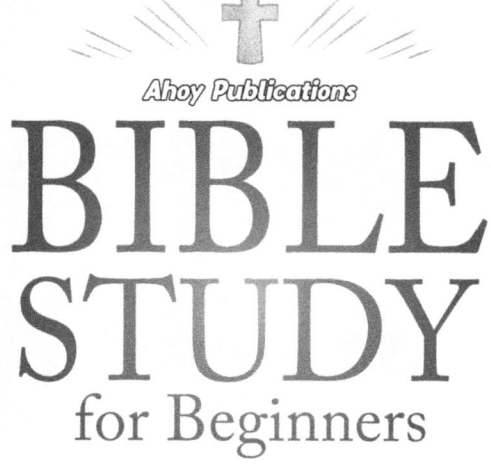

BIBLE STUDY
for Beginners

Unlocking the Essentials with
Beginner-Friendly and Easy-to-
Understand Explanations

Welcome Aboard, Check Out This Limited-Time Free Bonus!

Ahoy, reader! Welcome to the Ahoy Publications family, and thanks for snagging a copy of this book! Since you've chosen to join us on this journey, we'd like to offer you something special.

Check out the link below for a FREE e-book filled with delightful facts about American History.

But that's not all - you'll also have access to our exclusive email list with even more free e-books and insider knowledge. Well, what are ye waiting for? Click the link below to join and set sail toward exciting adventures in American History.

<u>Access your bonus here</u>
<u>https://ahoypublications.com/</u>
<u>Or, Scan the QR code!</u>